fast
thinking.
difficult
people

C000056581

PEARSON EDUCATION LIMITED

Head Office:
Edinburgh Gate
Harlow CM20 2JE
Tel: +44 (0)1279 623623
Fax: +44 (0)1279 431059

London Office:
128 Long Acre
London WC2E 9AN
Tel: +44 (0)20 7447 2000
Fax: +44 (0)20 7240 5771
Website: www.business-minds.com

———————————

First published in Great Britain in 2001

ISBN 0 273 65307 5

British Library Cataloguing in Publication Data
A CIP catalogue record for this book can be obtained from the British Library

10 9 8 7 6 5 4 3 2 1

Typeset by Pantek Arts Ltd, Maidstone, Kent.
Printed and bound in Great Britain by Ashford Colour Press, Hampshire

The Publishers' policy is to use paper manufactured from sustainable forests.

fast
thinking:
difficult
people

- ▶ **avoid confrontation**
- ▶ **deal with the problem**
- ▶ **improve the atmosphere**

by Ros Jay

contents

introduction

Life moves fast enough these days to keep you working at break-neck speed most of the time. What you can really do without is problem people who create unpleasantness and difficulties and just plain slow you down. Just because you didn't handle touchy Tessa just right, she's stalling on the paperwork you need. One wrong word to sulky Steven, and he won't give you the information to complete your report. And a simple misunderstanding with cranky Colin is causing ridiculous delays on the new contract.

In this age of fast working, difficult people cause delays and extra effort that you simply can't afford. Unfortunately, these people aren't suddenly going to change personality overnight. So you're going to have to do the work instead. And it's not so bad really. Once you know the techniques for handling these people, you'll find it comes naturally before long. Whether they are domineering, or they constantly pass the buck, whether they are sulkers or just plain whingy, there are techniques for getting the best from everyone and making your own job a damn sight easier.

This book is about difficult people wherever you encounter them at work, whether they are colleagues, bosses or your own team members. Most of the guidelines for handling them are much the same whatever their position – it's the person who is difficult, after all, not their role. But where there are different techniques, we'll highlight them.

Whoever is making your already hectic life more stressful, you simply want to know how to keep them out of your hair politely, so as not to cause any more hassle to yourself or anyone else. You just want:

 tips for dealing with any type of difficult personality

 shortcuts for getting what you want out of people fast

 checklists to make sure you haven't overlooked anything

… all put together clearly and simply. And short enough to read fast, of course.

So don't panic. Next time you see a colleague bearing down on you along the corridor red in the face with anger, or you catch two of your team members coming to blows, simply whip out this

book and give yourself a crash course in handling the situation with diplomacy and assurance. And still getting the result you want, of course. This book will tell you everything you need to know about handling the tough cookies in the tin; you'll even find a lightning crash course for handling difficult people in five minutes at the back of the book, if you're seriously pushed for time.

This book will take you through the six key stages or groups of skills for dealing with difficult people, from bosses and colleagues to your own team members:

1 To begin with, you need to identify exactly what you're trying to achieve when you attempt to deal with difficult people – not quite as obvious as it might seem.
2 After this, we'll look at the underlying strategies for making all encounters with difficult people more pleasant and straightforward, including feedback techniques, and simply being more assertive without winding anyone up.
3 Next, we'll look at some of the basic types of behaviour that create difficult situations, such as anger, silent sulks and emotional blackmail.
4 Chapter 4 is all about handling difficult bosses – it can be a lot more nerve-wracking than dealing with other difficult people, but it's easy once you know how.
5 Sometimes the real problem is conflict between members of your team, rather than yourself and someone else. So here's the low-down on sorting out other people's squabbles and personality clashes.
6 Finally, Chapter 6 gives you a whistle-stop guide to handling over 20 of the most common difficult types, from prima donnas to rule-benders.

This book will tell you everything you need to know about handling the tough cookies in the tin

fast thinking
gambles

This book is all about thinking on your feet: handling difficult people fast so you can concentrate your time on your core activities. But throughout the book, you'll find hints on how to handle difficult people next time – when you can allow yourself a little more time. So what's the point? Why not handle them as fast as possible every time?

Well, there's always an element of risk in doing anything at break-neck pace and giving yourself no leeway. Nineteen times out of 20 the guidelines and tips in this book will get you what you need out of people without wasting time. But just occasionally, a little more time will gain you a greater benefit. Let's look at a few examples:

- Some of these techniques will give you just the solution you want. But some may give you only a short-term solution to a potentially permanent problem. If you want to find a lasting solution, it can take a little longer (as you'll find out later).

- People can't change their personalities, but they can change their behaviour – if they want to. The fastest way to deal with a difficult person may be a technique that removes the problem from your point of view. But persuading the person to change their behaviour (which may take longer) can ease the problem for your team members and colleagues too – enabling everyone to work more effectively.

- Just because you've overcome the problem thrown up by your difficult workmate doesn't mean to say that you necessarily feel good about it. You may be left with a feeling of irritation and frustration. Another solution – albeit a more time-consuming one – might have left you feeling happier.

So when time is tight (and when isn't it?), you'll find this book full of great techniques as well as being a handy reference guide. But if ever the workload eases up for a few moments, find a chance to follow the advice on finding more lasting answers to some of the people problems that you encounter regularly. That way, you'll remove much of the need for quick-fix solutions.

1 your objective

This book promised you speed, and now we're messing about with fancy thing like objectives. It's a rip-off, that's what it is.

Actually, no. This isn't highfalutin' theory, it's real work. Setting your objective is as important to achieving success as getting out the road map before you embark on a long car journey to a new destination. In fact, it's very similar. Your objective *is* your destination, and without it you will be lost.

If you set off in your car and just follow your nose, the odds on ending up precisely where you want to are pretty slim. How can you possibly decide which route to take if you don't know where you're going? In the same way, when it comes to dealing with difficult people, if you don't know what you're trying to achieve, you can't have any idea how to go about it.

STOP, LOOK, LISTEN

The more rushed you are, the more worthwhile it is to take time out to set your objective. It doesn't take long, but it does ensure that you focus on the real issues. It's very easy when you're under time pressure to act rather than think, but this just leads to undirected – and therefore wasted – time and energy. So stop, set your objective, and then proceed.

So, we begin by setting an objective. It won't take long – three or four minutes. About as long as it takes to read this chapter, in fact. Once it's done, you'll know where you're going with all the other techniques in this book.

And what is your objective? Well, here are some possible outcomes to handling difficult people:

▶ **You get them out of your hair but you don't get what you need from them work-wise.**

▶ **You get your immediate problem resolved, but you leave them feeling angry and resentful (uh-oh, sounds like trouble ...).**

▶ **You keep them happy, but it takes the whole afternoon just to get a simple piece of information out of them.**

Setting your objective is as important to achieving success as getting out the road map before you embark on a long car journey to a new destination

▶ **You've broken up the row between your team members for the moment, but you know it's only a matter of time before they fall out again.**

In all of these cases, you have dealt with the difficult people, but none of them sounds like a perfect solution. Either it takes too long, or it's storing up trouble for later, or the people are fine but the work has suffered. So you need to set yourself a clear objective that resolves *all* these related problems, not just some of them.

When it comes to dealing with people problems, here's the sort of objective you need to aim for, at least if you're working at the speed of life: *To resolve the situation swiftly and permanently, in a way that meets work objectives and satisfies everyone involved.* That's more like it. Now you know where you're trying to get to, and you know you haven't succeeded until you have met the objective in full.

If this is a relatively minor problem, and you need to resolve it fast, you can use the objective outlined here. But if you have a serious people problem, or one that could cause major disruption to work, it's worth taking the time to spell out your objective in a little more detail. In particular, you should specify:

▶ the key work objectives
▶ what it will take to satisfy everyone.

For example, your objective might be: *To resolve the situation swiftly and permanently in a way that doesn't delay the report, and that leaves Richard feeling he has been given responsibility without Pat feeling displaced.* A detailed objective such as this will help you to keep focused on the outcomes that are important without getting sidetracked.

2 the basic techniques

You'll be pleased to know that there are certain underlying techniques that, once learnt, you can apply to most difficult people. Yes, it does take a short time to learn them initially, but the investment is worth it. They will then help you resolve numerous problems with such ease that you will barely notice there was a problem – now that's fast thinking.

LEOPARDS DON'T CHANGE THEIR SPOTS

Before you can learn anything about handling difficult people, however, you have to understand one critical thing about them: you can't change them. That is to say, you can't change their intrinsic personality. And once you accept that, you find that your tolerance level shoots up. Someone who used to be difficult now appears simply to be different from you. But before you despair, there is something you can change. You can — with their cooperation — get them to change their behaviour.

Let's take an example from outside work. When you're at home, are you a tidy person or an untidy one? Most couples who live together differ in this to some extent, and it's a frequent cause of arguments. One thinks the other is trying to make them live in a pigsty, and the other thinks their partner is creating unnecessary stress, and if they'd just relax they'd see it wasn't that important. So the tidy one tries to turn their partner into a tidy person — which creates resentment. Meanwhile, the other tries to make their tidy partner into a more laid-back kind of person who isn't really bothered about whether the towels live on the towel rail or on the bathroom floor. The tidy partner is angry at this attempt to change them.

thinking smart

ON TOLERANCE

I don't mean to sound preachy here, but it can help to think about ways in which you yourself might be classed as difficult — maybe at home, at work, or even by your mother. Are you neurotically tidy? Opinionated? Indecisive? Picky about food? Your difficult co-workers can no more change than you can, and probably no more see why they should than you do. Think on it.

The fact is, we can't change. If we could, we would do it and save the arguments. But because we *think* we can change the other person, we're upset and annoyed when they don't change. Our expectations of creating the kind of person we want aren't being met.

How about a different approach? Suppose we accept that we can't change the other person, so we stop trying. However, we can encourage them to adapt their behaviour. So, if you're the tidy one, try saying: 'I know you're not a tidy person. Could you, sometimes, be a messy person who puts the towels back on the rail?' It helps to be specific about your requests, and to limit them to a maximum of two or three at a time. This has two effects:

1 You have lowered your expectations, and no longer expect 100 per cent tidiness from them, so you'll be happier to settle for only 75 per cent.
2 They feel you're accepting them for what they are, so they have no need to feel angry or resentful.

This principle applies equally at work. If you try to change people, you create resentment and frustration on all sides when it doesn't work. But if you accept each other's intrinsic nature and work

SHARING TASKS

Accepting that people won't change can lead to all sorts of other solutions – because you can now have a friendly discussion where you both accept the other one's standpoint. This often leads, for example, to divvying up tasks differently. When it comes to tidying the bathroom, for example, it's not that big a deal to hang up their towels for them on the odd occasions they forget – and in exchange, they can do a couple of the jobs you really hate, like cleaning the hair out of the basin U-bend when the plughole won't drain.

with it, everyone feels understood and respected – the first and biggest step to cooperation.

STOCKING UP ON SKILLS

So how can we build on this new, more tolerant approach to difficult people? What techniques will help persuade them to cooperate by changing their behaviour? Well, a lot of the work has to come from you. Presumably, the person concerned is happy to be difficult (that's if they even recognize that they are), or they would change their behaviour without being asked. Perhaps their behaviour suits them very well. If they are

If you try to change people, you create resentment and frustration on all sides when it doesn't work

domineering, for example, and it seems to get them what they want, why should they change?

Even if they would prefer to be more popular, perhaps they feel unable to let go of their difficult traits. Maybe they don't feel comfortable behaving any other way – they are happier staying as they are.

Assertiveness

So you're going to have to make a fair bit of the running if things are going to change. And to do that, you need to arm yourself with the necessary skills. The first thing that many of us lack when it comes to difficult people is assertiveness. There are plenty of difficult types around, and some of them cannot be dealt with effectively unless you can be assertive with them. How about:

- the team member who constantly criticizes you

- the team member who likes to get their own way by shouting and losing their temper

- the colleague who begs more favours than you have time for – and makes it extremely hard to say no

- the senior colleague who talks over your head, blinds you with jargon, or treats you with impatient irritation if you don't grasp their ideas instantly

- the boss who never asks for your opinion or takes your views into account, even on projects you're heavily involved in

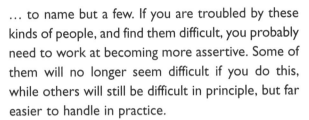

Being assertive is all about treating others as equals, and recognizing your own right to be treated as an equal by other people

- the boss who is always putting you down in front of other people

... to name but a few. If you are troubled by these kinds of people, and find them difficult, you probably need to work at becoming more assertive. Some of them will no longer seem difficult if you do this, while others will still be difficult in principle, but far easier to handle in practice.

Being assertive is all about treating others as equals, and recognizing your own right to be treated as an equal by other people. They may be senior to you in the company hierarchy, but they should still recognize that we are all created equal as people. If they don't, your assertiveness will put them straight – or at least ensure that they behave accordingly whatever their private views.

Once you begin to behave more assertively, people will begin to show you more respect. You must have noticed how submissive people are often overlooked, even when their contribution is valuable. And dominant characters get listened to more, regardless of whether what they are saying is worth hearing or not. Assertive people fall between these two extremes: they neither dominate others nor allow themselves to be dominated.

NO, BUT ...

When people ask favours that you simply don't have time for, say no with a very brief explanation: 'I'm sorry, I simply can't. I have to have this report finished by Thursday.' It's the guilt that often makes it hard for us to say no, so alleviate this by offering a suggestion or solution: 'Have you asked Meg? She's really good at that sort of thing.' At least you've shown your desire to help. (One thing: if you direct them towards someone else, pick on someone assertive enough to say no if they want to.)

So how do you do this assertiveness stuff? You're naturally slightly shy or underconfident, your mother brought you up to apologize even when it's the other person's fault, and now you want to change your behaviour. Well, there are three basic guidelines to being assertive:

▷ *Express your feelings.* **An assertive person must be able to say how they feel, good or bad. You don't want to upset people, but you have rights too. If someone else is upsetting you or making you angry, say so. Don't be unpleasant or inflammatory about it; simply say, for example, 'I feel angry when you don't allow me to express my view.' If you start by saying 'I feel ... when you ... ' you are far less likely to provoke conflict.**

- *Be honest.* You are allowed to say what you think. From 'I disagree' to 'I have reservations about your idea; I think it needs reconsidering.' This means you can criticize people, but being honest means you must do it fairly. Don't just be rude. But if you are still learning to be truly assertive, you're not likely to take your comments too far.

- *Stand your ground.* Don't be intimidated into backing down. If you are put under pressure to change something you're not willing to, simply keep repeating yourself, politley but firmly. If, for example, a colleague tries to persuade you to support their idea (which you actually think is dreadful) at a forthcoming meeting, just say 'I'm sorry, I can't support it.' If they continue to insist, repeat 'I'm sorry, I'd like to be able to support it, but I can't.' Stand your ground and don't be bludgeoned.

Assertive behaviour will not instantly resolve every difficult encounter, but it will have two key effects:

- It will reduce the number of people problems you have at work.

- It will enable you to stand up for yourself when difficult people need dealing with.

As a matter of fact, you'll find that all the techniques in this book are assertive techniques for handling difficult people. They are neither aggressive nor submissive, but show equal respect to you and to the person you're dealing with.

An assertive person must be able to say how they feel, good or bad

PRACTICE MAKES PERFECT

It will take months of practice to feel truly assertive, but you'll get there. Start by being assertive with easier colleagues, or over minor points. Once you feel comfortable and confident, begin to assert yourself with more difficult types or in more emotionally charged situations.

Keeping calm

Another of the basic techniques you need in your repertoire for handling difficult people is the ability to keep calm even when you are irritated, angry or upset. Some people can generate a strong emotional reaction – which is often entirely justified – but showing your emotions is never going to resolve the problem quickly or effectively. It is far more likely to lead to conflict and a build-up of animosity.

That is not to say that you should never express your emotions. As we've seen, the assertive approach is to let the other person know how their behaviour makes you feel. But you should let them know with words, not with a flood of tears or a torrent of rage. That way, you can phrase it so that they don't become defensive but are more likely to cooperate.

Face it. If someone starts hurling abuse at you or bursting into tears in response to behaviour that you feel is entirely reasonable and justified on your part, you are more likely to become defensive and resentful, and therefore far less willing to resolve their problem. So stay calm. Some of us find this easier than others, but keep your mind focused on your objective, and recognize that this is the way to get what you want with the minimum of hassle and time.

Feedback

Feedback is a specific technique for addressing problems with other people in a nonconfrontational way. One of the big advantages of this is that it's a relatively easy way to approach someone, so you don't have to wait until you're at breaking point before you tackle them.

Feedback works especially well with persistent problems, which is what you tend to encounter with difficult people. Suppose you have someone on your team who is a persistent complainer. Talk to them in private, when neither of you is in a particular hurry. Here's how you can use the rules of feedback to resolve the problem:

COUNT TO TEN

If you are so riled that you cannot speak calmly and rationally to the other person, just extract yourself from the conversation altogether until you have calmed down. Say something along the lines of, 'I don't feel happy about this. I'll talk to you about it later,' and then leave. If you can't leave, just shut up (and count to ten under your breath). If you're too emotional to speak calmly, don't speak at all.

1 Decide in advance the key points that you want to make, and prepare ways of saying them that do not include:

- exaggeration, such as 'you're always complaining'

- judgements, such as 'you're hopeless at dealing with problems yourself'

- labels, such as 'you're a whinger.'

2 When you speak to the person, focus on yourself and not them. Don't start sentences with 'You make me feel … '; try saying, 'I feel … when you … .' For example, 'I feel helpless and frustrated when you complain about things that I feel are minor details.'

3 Explain why you feel this way: 'I can't deal with them myself because I have other claims on my time that take higher priority; but I feel helpless having to say no to you.'

4 Now let the other person have their say. Listen to them, and show you're listening.

5 Focus on how they *behave*, not what they (in your view) *are*.

7 Be prepared to quote actual instances wherever possible.

8 Suggest a solution and see how the other person feels. This is very important; as we saw in the introduction, you can't change people's personalities, only their behaviour. So you must have an alternative behaviour in your mind that you are asking them to adopt. If you can't think of any solutions, you'd be better off not tackling the matter in the first place. Remember, you're not asking them to stop being a complaining

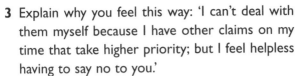

thinking smart

THE BIGGER PICTURE

If the person you are talking to is a member of your team, relate their behaviour to the task: point out how their behaviour is impairing the team's ability to get results.

person – they can't do that – you're asking them (perhaps not in so many words) to be a complainer who doesn't complain about certain things or at certain times. For example: 'Could you suggest a solution when you explain the problem to me? Try to think of something that doesn't involve time or resources that aren't available. Then, when you talk to me, I'll be better able to help and you'll find the complaint is more likely to be dealt with effectively.'

9 Listen to the other person's response and be prepared to compromise with them. (You may even learn something about how *you* appear to others, and be able to adapt your own behaviour and improve your performance.)

Many difficult people can be handled simply by using assertive behaviour, or by using the techniques we'll look at in Chapter 6 for individual types of difficult people. But when these approaches don't get the results you want, you can use feedback with any problem to meet your objective of resolving it swiftly and permanently, in a way that meets work objectives and satisfies everyone involved.

thinking smart

GIVE THEM THE GOOD NEWS

When dealing with your own team, be positive as well. Tell them when they have done well by not complaining, or whatever the problem behaviour is. Show them they *can* behave cooperatively.

When you have more time to reflect on the people problems around you, there's one scary question you need to consider: could it possibly be – even just sometimes – that the problem is you? Some people seem to have more difficult people problems than others, and this can be a good indicator that at least part of the problem lies with that person themselves.

So here's a private little checklist for you to run through. You never have to tell anyone you even bothered to glance through it. But just for reassurance …

Which of the following lists of personality traits would you say most closely describes you? Be honest, now, or the exercise is pointless.

List A	List B
You are good at seeing things from the other point of view	You have a strong, commanding tone
You don't interrupt people	You interrogate people firmly
You express yourself assertively	You have a loud speaking voice
You have a sincere tone of voice	You sometimes threaten people
When you ask questions, you listen attentively to the answers	You raise problems even when you have no solutions to them
You enjoy change	You take things personally
	You judge other people
	You don't always plan ahead

There are no prizes for recognizing that problem people mostly possess character traits in list B. Mind you, we're all a mixture of both lists – the question is which list describes you most predominantly? If you recognize yourself frequently in List B, try to work on the behaviours it describes (without changing your personality, of course), and see if you can't tone it down. You don't want other people going out and buying this book to help them deal with you.

And by the way, if you identified with every point on List A and none on List B, you must be a saint. And they're the worst of all to work with.

Could it possibly be – even just sometimes – that the problem is you

3 tricky types of behaviour

OK, you've learnt the basic techniques for handling problem people. You're going to be assertive from now on, you're going to keep calm (or go away and come back calm), and you know how to use feedback if you need to.

Some difficult people have a particular recurring characteristic that drives you mad, and we'll be looking at those in Chapter 6. But there are certain types of tricky behaviour that almost anyone can exhibit. Some people exhibit them regularly, and some only occasionally. Whichever is the case, they can come at you out of the blue, so you need to be ready to deflect them instantly. That way, you can meet your objective of resolving the problem swiftly and permanently, in a way that meets work objectives and satisfies everyone involved.

So what are these behaviours? The key ones, which I'm sure you'll recognize, are:

- ▶ **anger**
- ▶ **silence**
- ▶ **emotional blackmail.**

ANGER

Some people are justified in getting angry – we all are from time to time. Others get angry frequently in order to bludgeon you into doing things their way. The way you handle these two types is very different, so we'll look at them separately.

Justified anger

I'm sure you never give anyone cause to get angry, but even so most of us have to deal with other people's anger occasionally. Maybe there's been a misunderstanding; maybe the system is unreasonable and you are its representative – who else are your team members going to take out their frustration on when the organization lets them down?

Anger is rarely the best way for anyone to get what they want; if they are dealing with someone reasonable, fair and sympathetic (like you), it is never the best way. But we're all human. The question is, how do you handle it and diffuse things as fast as possible?

▶ People who get angry for a good reason do so because they feel they cannot get the response they want without getting angry. Usually they feel they are not being listened to. So the first thing to do is to listen to what they have to say. Hear them out, and they will begin to calm down.

▶ Show the person that you sympathize with their point of view. You may not be able to give them what they want, but you can still indicate that you appreciate their feelings. You can use phrases such as 'I can see that must be frustrating for you,' or 'No wonder you're feeling angry about it.'

▶ Don't wind them up by trying to justify your actions. It sounds as if you're making excuses, and are more interested in your side of the matter than theirs. Maybe they really need to know if their holiday dates have been approved before they can book their favourite hotel – which is about to become fully booked. And they've asked you twice already. The last thing they want to hear is a long explanation of how busy you've been and how difficult it is to schedule everyone's holidays.

▶ What angry people really want is a result. So the next step is to agree a resolution that they are happy with. Promise you'll do the dates by the end of the week; agree that if they miss their hotel thanks to you, you'll let them change their holiday time. Best of all, give them a choice – then they feel you've given them a measure of control: 'I'll do the dates by the end of the week but, if you prefer, I'll let you submit a different set of dates.'

thinking smart

KEEP YOUR PROMISES

Whatever you agree, stick to it. If you don't, you'll be dealing with someone twice as angry next time. And quite right too.

Tactical anger

People who lose their temper in order to intimidate you into giving in to them are an entirely different matter. The worst thing you can do is to let them get away with it. If it works, they'll keep doing it to you, and everyone else.

The first thing you need to do is to brush up on your assertiveness skills. You'll need them. You mustn't allow yourself to be intimidated, and you're not paid to be shouted at by someone who has never grown up. You may also find that feedback (following the guidelines in Chapter 2) works with this person. But before you try that, here are a few tips:

- ▶ **Don't allow yourself to be shouted or ranted at. Be assertive and say something along the lines of, 'I don't like being shouted at, and I shall leave if you don't calm down.'**

You're not paid to be shouted at by someone who has never grown up

KEEP A LID ON IT

Never respond to anger with anger. It doesn't work, it inflames the situation, it makes a resolution to the problem far less likely, it stores up resentment and bad feeling, and it loses you the moral high ground. So bite your tongue before you're tempted to bite their head off.

▸ **If they continue, do just that: leave. Say, 'I'll talk to you when you've calmed down,' or, if you find that hard to say, just say, 'Excuse me,' and walk out of the room.**

▸ **Continue this response at any subsequent encounters where they get angry, until they learn to talk to you rationally and reasonably.**

SILENCE

People sulk because they want to let you know how upset they are. If they didn't sulk (they feel), you would think the matter wasn't important to them. Almost all of us are prone to sulk occasionally, but some people do it over such seemingly minor issues that it ends up happening frequently and creates an unpleasant and unhelpful attitude that can seriously sour the working relationship. Whether you are dealing with a regular sulker or an unexpected dose of the silent treatment, the guidelines for handling it are the same.

- Silence is intended to make you feel guilty once you realize how upset the person is. Any approach to handling a sulker works only if you honestly have nothing to feel guilty about. So when you have the kind of discussion with this person that can lead to an unpleasant silence, make sure you genuinely listen to them with an open mind, explain the reasons behind your view of the matter, and act in a friendly and reasonable way. Once the discussion is over, if they choose to sulk you know that there is nothing else you could have done except give in for no good reason, simply to avoid it.

- The aim is that you will capitulate. Never, ever do so. If it works for them once, they will try it every time.

- Don't perpetuate the atmosphere by being short with them either. Behave as if everything were normal. If they give you the silent treatment, just say 'OK, we'll sort it out later.' If it really can't wait, force them to answer you. Ask them the question and then wait for their response. And wait ... and wait. Force them to break the silence by answering – it's their turn to speak after all. Once you've shown them that you can hold out longer than them, they won't try that technique again.

CHECK THE FACTS

Remember that most of us sulk to some extent over major issues when we feel our feelings aren't being taken seriously. Even frequent sulkers occasionally have a genuine case – they really aren't being listened to or considered over something important. So always make a mental check when they get upset and satisfy yourself that this isn't one of those occasions – or if it is, hear them out.

EMOTIONAL BLACKMAIL

'I'm going to be in a real mess if you don't help me out with this.' 'Don't give me a hard time for being late, I find it so difficult to get up in the mornings.' 'Please don't be uncooperative.' Emotional blackmail is a popular weapon for getting people to do whatever the blackmailer wants. They are playing on your guilt, or your desire to be popular, in order to manipulate you into doing things their way.

But there's one thing you need to know about emotional blackmail: it doesn't work on assertive people. And the emotional blackmailers learn to recognize assertive people and they stop using this insidious technique on them. So apply a bit of assertiveness and become impervious to this kind of manipulation.

- Recognize emotional blackmail for what it is. As soon as you start to feel guilty about saying no, or emotionally uncomfortable about your response to someone, ask yourself, 'Am I being emotionally blackmailed?' Once you're alerted to the possibility, you'll have no trouble recognizing when it's happening.

- Tell yourself that emotional blackmail is not a fair, equal, adult behaviour, and that you owe nothing to those who use it. If they're prepared to use such an underhand approach with you, you are quite entitled to respond by not giving in to it.

- Now simply stand your ground, according to the assertiveness guidelines in the previous chapter. If they persist, adopt the stuck record technique. Don't allow them to make you feel bad – it is they who are behaving unreasonably, not you.

- Challenging people directly over this technique can cause unpleasantness, but with some people you may find that you can say – with a joke and a laugh – 'Careful! That's starting to sound like emotional blackmail … ' It pulls them up short. If they think you're getting wise to them they'll back off.

There's one thing you need to know about emotional blackmail: it doesn't work on assertive people

◀◀ for next time

Once you get used to using these techniques – and you may encounter these behaviours often enough to get plenty of practice – you'll find they get easier and easier to handle. The key is to recognize them early, and nip them in the bud:

▶ As soon as someone starts to sulk, simply leave them alone. Don't give them the satisfaction of knowing that you've even noticed.

▶ Recognize someone else's mounting anger before it goes too far, and stop yourself responding in kind.

▶ Learn to recognize emotional blackmail as soon as it rears its head, and don't allow yourself to be taken in and to start feeling guilty.

Recognize someone else's mounting anger before it goes too far, and stop yourself responding in kind

4 difficult bosses

In some ways, problem bosses are the most difficult of all to deal with. You inevitably worry because they have the power to influence your career, and whatever you do you don't want to upset them. This is a perfect example of where you really do need fast thinking to keep them sweet *and* get what you need from them too.

You'll find that many difficult bosses exhibit traits that you also find in colleagues and team members. If this is the case, you will probably find all the tips you need elsewhere in this book. But there are some difficult characteristics that are only – or chiefly – a problem when you find them in your boss. And that's what this chapter is about.

There are three main types of behaviour that fall into this category – see if you recognize any of these bosses:

- ▶ **the one who never backs you up**
- ▶ **the one who breathes down your neck**
- ▶ **the one who's always right**

THE BOSS WHO NEVER BACKS YOU UP

These people are often friendly, affable and easy to get along with. But when you need a decision made, or need someone to put your case to senior management – or even just need advice – they somehow wriggle, stall, or just plain disappear. They are the enemy of fast thinking.

Often, the problem is that they simply can't handle conflict. So, rather than tell you that your proposal isn't considered good enough to implement, they just avoid making a decision on it. Or worse, they send you off to do some extra research on it, or add another section, just to put off having to disappoint you.

And it's not only you they don't want to get into deep water with. They are nervous of arguing with their own bosses. So when you ask them to clear a budget increase for you, they somehow never sort it out. They take no for an answer without putting up any reasoned defence, and leave you in an impossible position.

There are some difficult characteristics that are only – or chiefly – a problem when you find them in your boss

Because they hate conflict, this boss is also very reluctant to give you constructive criticism or to put you straight if you go wrong. Consequently, you may well have little idea if your performance isn't up to scratch. This is demoralizing for you, and can be downright dangerous to your career if more senior managers can see the problem but your own boss hasn't enlightened you.

So what can you do to get these reluctant bosses to start doing their job properly? Here are a few techniques that will help:

- If you ask them for a straight opinion on your performance, they won't be able to make any negative comments. It might upset you. They'll just insist there's nothing wrong. So if you sense there's a problem, try phrasing your question differently: 'What do you think could improve my proposal to make it even better?' This allows them to feel they are being helpful rather than brutally honest, and they answer while still implying that the proposal was excellent.

- If your boss is stalling, there is some kind of conflict. Maybe they know that senior management don't want to see any budget increases this year. Or maybe they feel that their own boss doesn't support the project you want the additional funds for. So get them to tell you what the conflict is; then you know what you're dealing with. And they may find it easier to tackle the situation once it's out in the open. Try saying, 'I realize there's a conflict for you

RESIST TEMPTATION

The temptation with these bosses is often to go over their heads simply to get a decision or an answer. But doing this will rile them, and could well cause more problems than it solves. So avoid this if you possibly can.

here. I'm pushing for a budget increase for this budget. So what's on the other side, holding you back?'

▶ If your boss is simply indecisive and puts off making decisions, try acting as an unofficial adviser, and see if you can't help them to find a firm solution. Or simply make the decision yourself. Talk to them about the problem, and then say 'That's really helpful. OK, I'll tell you what I'll do ... ' Make this a statement rather than a question. This gives them the chance to disagree, but almost certainly they will leave you to get on with it, having effectively approved your decision.

▶ Don't pressure this kind of boss too hard. If the pressure feels worse to them than the risk of doing something, they will do anything just to get you off their back. And it probably won't be what you want them to do.

THE BOSS WHO BREATHES DOWN YOUR NECK

There are few things more frustrating at work than being denied the responsibility you know you can handle because your boss won't let go. Very possibly it's responsibility you actually hold on paper, but in reality you can't make a move without your boss's express approval.

These people may be control freaks, power hungry, perfectionists or just plain paranoid that you'll get more credit than them. Whatever their particular motivation, they need to be dealt with swiftly so you can get on with doing your job properly – by yourself.

- Check that you aren't doing something that gives your boss cause (however unjustified) to check up on you. If they don't seem willing to let you make decisions, or they seem to mistrust your expenses claims, ask them – without being defensive – what their reason is. For example, 'I realize you don't always trust my judgement. It would be helpful if you would tell me the reason.' Then sit back and wait for the response. You might not like it, but listen anyway.

- Once you've heard them out, acknowledge their worries even if they seem unfounded to you. Then you can reassure them that it won't happen again – with some concrete reason why it won't: 'I can understand why you've been concerned in the past. But I've devised a new monitoring system now ... '

- Try to emulate your boss more. I know that sounds like a recipe for madness, but the point is that if they think you work in the same way they do, they are more likely to trust you. So include the same level of detail in your reports

that they do in theirs, and try to use the same approach as them to problem-solving or handling tricky situations.

THE BOSS WHO'S ALWAYS RIGHT

This boss won't listen to anyone else's point of view. Why should they? They already know the right answer. And once they've made up their minds about something (which doesn't generally take long) the subject is closed. Full stop.

Although this boss doesn't breathe down your neck, they have a similar constricting effect because they know exactly how to do your job, and they won't be happy if you don't do it the way they know is right. Here are the best ploys for dealing with the boss who's always right.

thinking smart

GO NATIVE

Don't get defensive, especially if there seems to be a level of personal mistrust (such as a conviction that you're fiddling your time sheet). Perversely, what you should do is encourage your boss to check up on you (no that wasn't a misprint – I really did say 'encourage'). The point of this is that it will build your boss's trust in you, and although they may take the opportunity initially, they are more likely to loosen their hold once they see that you are trustworthy.

▷ Never tell them they're wrong. You've probably picked this one up already, but what do you do when they are wrong? The best way to get them to see it is by asking innocent questions: 'Can you explain how that will work in peak production periods?' 'I think I follow, but what happens after the initial promotion?' 'Could you just explain how that works with new staff?' Now sit back, and let your boss realize their error of judgement for themselves.

▷ If you have trouble wresting responsibility away from this expert who knows how to do the job so much better than you, be realistic. Find the area of the job they find least interesting or consider least important, and ask to be allowed to make decisions over that. For example, 'I know Scotland is our smallest territory, and none of our big customers are there. Could I look after those regional accounts, with authority to agree discounts? There won't be any really big figures involved anyway, and I've been watching the way you handle customer discounts in the south-east.' This way you can slowly build up a recognition in them that you know much of what they do, and must therefore be right quite often yourself.

▷ Make sure you get things right as often as is humanly possible. Do your homework thoroughly, so that your results always demonstrate that you, too, are invariably right. Well, almost ... you'll doubtless find that no one else is allowed to be quite perfect.

thinking smart

NEVER GLOAT

Bosses who are always right, and therefore never listen to anyone else, are actually wrong quite often (surprise, surprise). When this happens, resist the temptation to say 'I told you so,' and instead help your boss to save face: 'Of course, if it hadn't been a leap year, your projections for February would have been spot on.' There's a good reason for this. These people, once proved wrong, will always look for someone else to blame. (Obviously. It couldn't have been them, after all, because they're always right.) So align yourself with them fast, so the finger of blame points past you and elsewhere.

for next time

Learn to spot difficult bosses further up the organization, so that you can either avoid working directly under them (if possible) or at least lay the groundwork for being the kind of person whose work they respect. Get on the right side of them now, and when the time comes, the job of taming them will be a whole load easier.

5 conflict in the team

As a team leader, you'll know that even if you are an expert at handling difficult people, you can still have problems when they aren't experts at handling each other. Conflict within the team is your problem, even when you are not one of the protagonists. What's more, it is a problem that can disrupt everyone and waste the whole team's time. So you need to be able to sort out conflict promptly and effectively.

The first thing to recognize is that there is less conflict in well-run teams than in poorly run teams, so if you're doing your job properly things will be easier from the kick-off. The key guidelines for maintaining a happy team are:

- Make sure everyone is doing a job that suits them and that they can enjoy.

- Make sure you are approachable and easy to talk to when your team members have problems.

- Ensure your team members are all well motivated (you'll find guidelines on motivation in *Fast Thinking: Project*).

- Make sure everyone in the team understands the objectives of their jobs, and the team's overall objective. As with any individual project, so each person should also have their own objective (see *Fast Thinking: Work Overload*).

- Help ease the stress for any team members who have personal problems (you'll find a section on counselling interviews in *Fast Thinking: Discipline*).

I'm sure all of these are second nature to you; they are core skills that all good managers possess. However, even the best-run team suffers occasional conflict, so how can you nip it in the bud? The most common ongoing problem is a personality clash within the team. You have to address the two people involved by sitting down with them and talking through the problem. You have to get them together, otherwise they will each wonder what you said to the other, and they may even misrepresent you to each other. This could make the problem worse rather than better, and it could even turn into a three-way conflict that you have become entangled in.

- Create a relaxed, informal setting to discuss the problem, at a time when no one is under time pressure.

- Make it clear from the start that your job is to focus on objectives and to ensure that the team works towards them as effectively as possible. Their conflict is inhibiting that process, and you want to resolve it for the sake of the team. Explain that you do not wish to allocate blame – you simply want to resolve the problem.

- Ask them to accept you as a mediator. Tell them that you believe that talking through the problem will resolve it, but get their agreement that if there are any points they cannot resolve they will accept your decision on them. These can always be reviewed later if the difficulties persist.

- Explain to them the techniques of feedback, which we looked at in Chapter 2. Tell them that you would like them to use the feedback format to discuss their conflict. Remind them that feedback rules state that they should each allow the other to finish what they are saying, focus on the problem and not each other's personality, and talk about their own feelings and reactions rather than focus on the other person's actions.

thinking smart

KEEP YOUR OPINIONS TO YOURSELF

Make absolutely sure that you give no indication whatever of any personal bias. If you think one of the team members is being more unreasonable or difficult than the other, don't let either of them see it. You are a referee only, so don't express an opinion.

- Keep out of the discussion as much as possible, except to remind them of the rules if they start to stray from them.

- Don't allow them to finish the meeting without an agreement – a verbal contract – about their future behaviour. If one person is in any way coerced into this arrangement they are unlikely to follow it, so you need to make sure that it is a genuinely mutual agreement. Make sure that one of them isn't making all the concessions in order to keep things sweet, but that they are both taking steps to meet each other half way.

- Do anything you can to help in your capacity as team leader. For example, they may ask you to reallocate certain tasks, or reprioritize them, or to rearrange the office layout so the two work physically closer together or further apart. You brought these two people together to resolve their differences, so it's important that you are seen to cooperate when it comes to taking practical steps to achieve that resolution.

thinking smart

FOLLOW IT UP

Arrange a date to review things after a few days or weeks (whichever seems appropriate). This way, no one feels they have to commit themselves to an arrangement that they might not be happy with once they have tried it, and if it only partly solves the problem they have a chance later to discuss further action. At the review session, thank them for any success they have had in making their solution work.

> At the end of the meeting, thank both of them for cooperating in trying to resolve the problem. Tell them you recognize that it isn't always easy, and that by managing to improve matters they have benefited the team as a whole.

FACTIONS WITHIN THE TEAM

There's one thing even worse than a personality clash between two members of the team, and that is when the entire team divides into factions. This is a major problem at the best of times, and when schedules are tight and deadlines are bearing down on you, it can become a waking nightmare.

If you have a well-managed team (and I'm sure you do), it's extremely unlikely your team will separate into factions. But it can occasionally happen to the best of us. In the unlikely event, you need to identify what kind of split it is. There are three factors that can cause a split in the team:

> disagreement over policy issues

> a status battle between two senior team members

> rivalry between groups in the team.

Each of these problems has a different choice of solutions, so we'll look them individually.

The policy issue split

There may be such strong disagreement in the team about the collective goal that it splits the group. For example, the team can't agree whether it should concentrate on the domestic or industrial market.

▸ **You need to identify the problem as early as you can (a standard fast thinking approach). In many cases, this is just a matter of not ignoring it in the hope it will go away. The sooner you take action, the better – and if you can pre-empt a split completely, that's even better. You can't act too soon.**

▸ **Call a team meeting and discuss the issues. The aim of the meeting is to reclarify the team's objectives. If you have built a strong team, its members will want to reach agreement and they will understand the importance of doing so. Your job is to make sure it happens.**

▸ **Once a decision has been made, you need to make it evident that it is final. There's no point in your team members continuing to discuss the merits and demerits of the various options because it's too late. So, whatever you do, don't let them think it's open for review later.**

▸ **It can help to follow up this session with an increased workload (within reason) or a major challenge to the team. You can often create this by bringing forward a project the team would normally have started work on in a few weeks' time. The object of the exercise is to unite the team in a common cause, and put them under just enough pressure that they don't have time to dwell on past decisions and emotions but focus on future plans instead.**

START A SMALL WAR

One of the best ways to unite the team is to focus them on threats, dangers, rivals or enemies outside the team. If you can make them feel that survival is at stake and the enemy is beating at the gates, internal disputes seem less important. It is on the same principle (if a little more dramatic) that dictators often start foreign wars to forestall revolution at home.

The status battle split

This can be a little tougher to deal with. What happens is that the factions form around two key players on the team who have different aims for the team, different styles of working, or different ambitions for themselves.

▶ **This situation can arise only if the two people involved are pulling in different directions. You need to refocus them on the team, its needs and its objectives.**

▶ **Call the two people together and mediate while they discuss their differences together, following the guidelines we have just covered.**

▶ **The greatest danger in this situation will come if you are weak in the way you handle it. You will need to be firm with these two people, and tell them that the split in the** team would not be happening unless they were allowing it to. Point out that the team is suffering as a result of the split, and that if they are committed to the team they must smooth out their differences and work to reunite the team.

 The most important question to address with these people is, 'What is the best way for the team to accomplish the task?' Once you retreat to 'What is the best way to keep A happy, or stop B sulking?' you are on a very slippery slope. People will realise that success depends on the force of their personalities not the force of their arguments.

The group rivalry split

This happens most commonly when there are already two groups within the team – say, national sales and international sales – or when the team is made up of two smaller teams that have been merged. In this case, a natural rivalry springs up between the two teams just as, when I was at

thinking smart

TELL IT LIKE IT IS

If a status battle split has reached a critical point, or the people involved are not willing to cooperate, it may well be necessary to point out that if they do not have the necessary commitment to the team there is no place for them as a member of it.

school, there was rivalry between the A stream and the B stream (despite the fact that we were streamed quite randomly, not according to ability).

> Don't assume this is necessarily a bad thing. Sometimes it encourages healthy competition. If you have, for example, two regional sales forces competing, you need to make sure that the atmosphere remains friendly, that one team doesn't become demoralized by always being seen as the 'losers', and that the rewards are designed to motivate but are not valuable enough to create serious jealousies.

thinking smart

GETTING TO KNOW YOU

Groups tend to have collective personalities. Other teams in the organization will be perceived as 'clever' or 'spoilt' or 'aggressive'. When two teams merge, each sees the members of the other team in this light. Encourage them to see each other as individuals and this feeling often dissipates. Try sitting members of each team at desks next to each other, organize team social events, hold regular team meetings and generally speed up the 'getting to know each other' stage. Hold contests at team social events in which the teams are mixed up, so that rivals become allies.

- Sometimes you can handle this a little differently and split the existing factions into smaller groups so that each competes with its previous 'allies' as well as with its previous 'opponents'.

- If the atmosphere has become tense and the rivalry is being taken too seriously, swap round some of the key people – have a reshuffle – so that they can't compete.

Team conflict is a worrying thing, since it eats into everyone's time and productivity. But with some fast thinking and smart action, you'll find that you can keep any difficulties to a minimum and get on with the things that really matter.

for next time

Make it standard practice to train your team members (not forgetting any new members who join) in feedback skills. That way, they may well be able to resolve minor conflicts themselves. And when you *do* have to get involved, you can address the problem straight away without having to take time to teach them the techniques for resolving it first.

6 the fast guide to problem people

Right. You're under pressure, the workload is mounting, the deadlines are getting tighter. And just as you're trying to get to grips with it all, someone turns up and starts causing problems. Or maybe they've always been difficult but it seems more of a problem now that you've got no time to deal with it. What you need is a handy reference guide for dealing with the most common problem types. So here it is.

Simply run through the contents list at the front of the book, and find the one you need. Then look it up in this chapter for some much needed tips on how to get them off your back. Sorry, I mean how to resolve the situation swiftly and permanently, in a way that meets work objectives and satisfies everyone involved.

THE UNCOMMUNICATIVE PERSON

Some people are naturally slow to contribute to conversations and may genuinely not realize how unhelpful they are being. One of the problems associated with this behaviour is that these people often fail to commit themselves to anything because they tend to speak in 'Mmms' and 'Uh-huhs' rather than using phrases such as 'I'll have it ready by Tuesday morning.' Consequently, they often infuriate their fellow team members who feel they can't rely on them. Feedback is often very effective, but before you try it, here are a few tips that may ease the situation:

- **Ask these people a lot of questions to encourage them to talk, and make the questions as specific as you can. So don't ask, 'Can you get this report done next week?'; try 'This report needs to be about 5000 words, and I need it on Thursday week at the latest. Will you be able to do that?'**

- **Except when eliciting commitments from them, ask open questions (ones to which they cannot reply 'yes' or 'no'). This forces them to communicate more.**

- Once you've asked a question, shut up and wait for them to answer. Don't feel uncomfortable – the onus is on them to speak first so tough it out.

THE PERSON WHO NEVER LISTENS

Don't you just hate 'em? These people can be incredibly frustrating for everyone. Not only do you know damn well they're not really listening while you're speaking to them, but tasks frequently don't get done as a result. And when you tackle them, they claim you never told them about it in the first place. There is, however, a simple technique for dealing with this:

- When you've finished speaking, say, 'I want to be certain I'm making this clear. Could you just repeat it back to me?'

- If you are worried they're repeating back to you parrot fashion and still won't remember, ask them questions – open ones, so they can't just say 'Mmm': 'What do you think about including case studies in the report, and how should we work them in if we use them?'

- These people will never remember what you did over the weekend – just concentrate on making sure they remember what they need to get the job done well.

THE DAYDREAMER

The problem with daydreamers is that their productivity drops when they start to dream, and

GET REAL

Don't expect to convert uncommunicative people into good communicators; you won't. Just encourage them to communicate enough for the rest of the team to be able to work with them comfortably.

When you've finished speaking, say, 'I want to be certain I'm making this clear. Could you just repeat it back to me?'

then they tend to make mistakes. As a result, they often let down their colleagues. The chief cause tends to be boredom, so the best treatment is to keep their attention going.

- ▶ Give them tasks to share with someone else – the other person will keep them awake and on their toes.

- ▶ As far as possible, let them decide which tasks they want to do when.

- ▶ Set them productivity targets paired with accuracy targets, and with good incentives for meeting them.

- ▶ Accept that these people will never be suited to certain kinds of monotonous work and try to avoid giving it to them.

THE LONER

Loners are happy that way. They like keeping their office door shut. The problem when they're on your team is that they aren't really team players. As a result, they can appear quite remote and often negative to the rest of the team, and can inhibit a free flow of ideas.

- **Loners tend to withdraw further if they are put under pressure to be social. As we've established already, you can't change them, so you might as well accommodate them. In fact, this will probably improve matters. Allow them their privacy and don't force them to attend large gatherings.**

- **Loners are often more comfortable talking to people on the phone than face-to-face. So call them on the internal phone sometimes instead of walking round to their office.**

THE SECRETIVE PERSON

Some people make a habit of keeping back information from the rest of the team, which makes it impossible for everyone to feel that

thinking smart

IT'S NOT ALL BAD

Recognize that loners have certain positive qualities: they tend to work well on their own, have a bent for detailed work, and can be very good at working on long-term projects. Exploit these talents, and make sure the rest of the team appreciates them as well – they may well be glad to pass these tasks on to someone who wants to do them.

they're pulling together. It helps to understand why people do this. There are two common reasons for it: one is that it gives them a feeling of power, and the the other is that they have a particularly strong need for recognition.

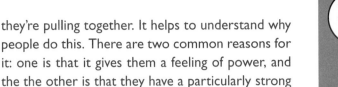 Make your requests for information very specific, and put them in writing if necessary.

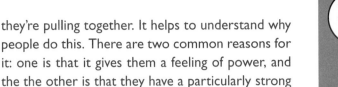 Alternatively, write down the information you already have and ask them to fill in the blanks for you; this should satisfy any need for power that they have. They'll get a feeling of satisfaction from being able to tell you what you didn't know.

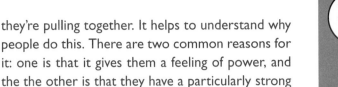 When they give you the information you wanted, be warm and generous with your thanks so they feel smart for having been able to supply it. Do this in front of other people when you can. This should satisfy their need to have their contribution acknowledged.

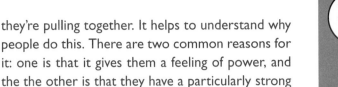 You should be able to tell from their reaction to these approaches which of the two reasons for being secretive applies in their case. Once you've worked out which of the approaches suits them best, you can concentrate on that. In future, you should have no problems getting information out of them.

THE OVERSENSITIVE PERSON

Every tiny criticism is taken as a personal slight with these people, making it almost impossible to discuss their work objectively. You'll always have to watch what you say, but there are ways to minimize the problem:

- **Never make any comment they could take offence at in front of other people; this will make them feel humiliated.**

- **Make sure that your criticisms are objective, specific and worded so as to be clearly critical of their work and not themselves. So don't say, 'I'm a bit worried about your performance lately'; say, 'I'm a bit worried that you've missed two deadlines in the last month.'**

- **Build their self-confidence. Always point out where they have done well when you discuss their weak points: 'Mind you, although you delivered the work a day late, it was a terrific report.' Comment on strengths of personality as well as work: 'You have a real knack for getting to the heart of an issue.'**

thinking smart

EASE UP

Remember that if people are very sensitive, a little criticism goes a long way. If you say, 'I'm a bit worried,' they'll feel they've turned in the worst month's work in history. If you say, 'I'm not satisfied with this report,' they'll be heading for the razor blades before you've finished the sentence. So go easy on them.

THE MARTYR

Martyrs are always taking on extra work and moaning about it. 'Still, someone's got to do it,' 'Go on, I'll add it to my in-tray,' 'Don't worry, I'll manage.' .... The problem with martyrs is that they often make other people feel guilty for not working as hard as them, and their tension and negativity can spread through the team. They are also very prone to stress, which is disruptive for them and their colleagues.

You can't convert a martyr into a laid-back, relaxed person. But you can minimize the disruption they cause around them:

▶ **Don't allow them to take on extra work. Keep their workload to a reasonable level and politely decline any offers to help out with urgent or extra tasks. Encourage them to take full lunch breaks and to go home on time.**

▶ **If necessary, have a private talk to tell them you're concerned about the stress they put themselves under. Make it clear to them that you don't expect them to take on extra work, and you won't think them any less able if they keep their workload down.**

▶ **You could tactfully point out that their effect on the rest of the team is counterproductive. Bear in mind, however, that martyrs are often extremely sensitive, so be very diplomatic. You could imply, for example, that others are inclined to feel inferior because they don't have the martyr's stamina, and that this damages morale.**

Remember that if people are very sensitive, a little criticism goes a long way

Martyrs often feel inadequate themselves and are driven by a need to prove their ability and boost their self-confidence. So make sure you give them plenty of recognition for the work they do. Reduce this slightly when they overwork, and shift it to concern for their health and the team's morale. They are more likely to prefer the response they get when they work less hard.

THE MOANER

There are two good points worth making about people who constantly complain (honest):

1 They will often be the ones who bring genuine problems to your attention – problems that you want to know about. Because of their natural tendency to moan, the team will often unofficially appoint them as spokesperson for the group, and when they come to you they may be airing a commonly held complaint.

2 They are often very conscientious workers. If they weren't, they wouldn't care when things went wrong. It's because they care that they complain.

Bear these points in mind when they come to you with their latest complaint. But to minimize the minor whinges they come to you with:

THE PRE-EMPTIVE STRIKE

Before they complain, ask them if they need any help. Occasionally, they may see this as an invitation to complain, but more often than not they will tell you things are fine (if they'd thought of a complaint they'd have voiced it already). Once they have committed themselves to the attitude that everything's OK, it makes it harder for them to start moaning later.

▶ **Don't make decisions that affect them directly without consulting them first. If they feel involved in any changes or new procedures they will feel less inclined to moan.**

▶ **Try to avoid putting them under pressure – this almost always leads this kind of person to complain.**

▶ **When they complain, these people are prone to keep analyzing the reasons why the problem has arisen. Focus them on the solution instead: 'Well, it's happened now. What do you think is the best way to resolve it?' Just occasionally, it may be useful to know the background so you can prevent the problem recurring, but even so, suggest to them: 'Let's identify the reason for the situation later; for now, let's just worry about resolving it.'**

Don't make decisions that affect complainers directly without consulting them first

THE PESSIMIST

When someone says, 'It'll never work,' it's extremely frustrating as well as being unconstructive. On the other hand, the pessimists are often the ones who stop the group from making mistakes. But they need careful handling to exploit their ability to spot flaws, and stop them dragging the team down.

▶ **When they express a negative view, ask them to make it specific. Why won't it work? Are they guessing or are they basing their assessment on the facts? Is it just a hunch or do they have previous experience of this sort of thing? Be firm about getting them to be precise about which part of the project will create difficulties and why.**

▶ **Ask them how they think the problem can be resolved. Again, get them to be specific. Don't settle for 'I don't know – the whole thing looks like a waste of time to me.'**

▶ **Pessimists are often afraid of failure, and therefore avoid taking risks. They try to stop the whole team taking risks as well by adopting a negative viewpoint. Try asking them to tell you what they think the worst possible scenario could be as a result of following the course of action under discussion. This process often helps them to get their feelings in perspective.**

▶ **Remove their fear of failure by relieving them of as much responsibility as possible. Then, even if the project does fail, it won't be *their* failure. Either tell them you will take responsibility for the decision, or make it clear that the team as a whole is responsible (which dilutes their**

personal ownership of the project). Often, with this burden lifted, pessimists can become helpful contributors – although they will never become optimists.

THE PREJUDICED PERSON

There are all sorts of prejudice you can encounter at work. The most commonly cited are sexism and racism, but some people dislike working for people younger than them, or sharing an office with someone from a different social background. You haven't a hope of persuading someone through reasoned argument to change this kind of attitude. Often the best way to resolve this kind of problem is the feedback approach outlined at the beginning of the chapter. But it is sometimes possible to change these sorts of behaviour without broaching the subject directly.

thinking smart

TURN THE TABLES

Don't get into arguments about whether women are as good as men, whether experience is everything, whether the immigration laws are too lenient, or whether all people educated at public school are snobs. Just remember, *you* have as much chance of convincing someone prejudiced of your point of view as *they* have of persuading you round to their way of thinking.

- ▶ **Show them they're wrong.** Let's take sexism as an example. If you have a sexist man on your team, make sure that the women on the team have the chance to demonstrate that their abilities aren't restricted by their sex. Give them traditionally male tasks to do. Once their sexist colleague sees they can do them perfectly well, their attitude may soften.

- ▶ **Make sure you don't inadvertently reinforce their prejudice** – you might want to talk about this to other team members who are affected. For instance, a woman who asks a sexist man to change the light bulb in her office is reinforcing his prejudice. It may be that she's only asking because she's not tall enough to reach it herself, but she still isn't doing her cause any good. Far better to stand on a chair and change the bulb herself, or at least wait until he's out of the office and then ask someone else.

THE JOBSWORTH TYPE

The jobsworth won't do anything that isn't down in black and white in their job description. These people can crush everyone else's collective motivation. Forget cooperation, forget mutual support – they're not interested. You need to find out why if you can. Often, jobsworths behave as they do because they feel unappreciated. If you thank them generously when they do you a favour they'll be more inclined to put themselves out for you next time. So how do you get them to do you the first favour?

- ▶ You need to appreciate, as they already do, that if it's not on their job description they don't have to do it. It's no good getting annoyed or frustrated. They're absolutely entitled to say no.

- ▶ They know the rule book and their own job description like the back of their hand, so you'd better know it too. Then, at least you'll know whether you're asking them to do something they're paid to do, or whether you're asking them a favour.

- ▶ If you're asking them to do something outside their remit, let them know that you know you're asking a favour. Don't say, 'Please get today's orders over to despatch.' Say, 'I know you're busy but Kim's off sick today and today's orders need to go over to despatch. Would you mind taking them?'

- ▶ If they say no, accept it gracefully. If you say, 'That's fair enough, it's not your job,' you're showing them that you respect their rights. This approach might at least soften them up for next time.

- ▶ If you want them to do you a favour, make it a two-way deal and thank and reward them for it.

- ▶ Some jobsworths behave as they do because they suffer from a deep insecurity and fear of the repercussions that will result if they make a mistake. It is therefore important that you don't bawl them out if they do slip up.

If you have a sexist man on your team, make sure that the women on the team have the chance to demonstrate that their abilities aren't restricted by their sex

LEARNING BY EXAMPLE

Encourage cooperation between all members of your team. The jobsworth may learn from the others' examples, and may sometimes be persuaded more easily by other members of the team than by you.

THE CONTROL FREAK

These people are so nervous of being let down that they find it virtually impossible to delegate or share work. This both frustrates and excludes their colleagues. They are often perfectionists and they need recognition – that's why they find being let down so painful. Control freaks cannot change their innate fear of being let down, but they can learn – in the right circumstances – to change their behaviour and delegate more work to others.

▷ These people are happy if they know they can trust people to work to as high a standard as they do. So allow them to delegate or share work at a more gradual rate than most people, so they can learn one step at a time that the people around them can be trusted.

▷ While they are learning this, encourage people to keep them posted as to what is going on, and ask their advice where necessary. This way, they are continually aware that the task is being carried out satisfactorily.

- (▶) If anyone around them makes a mistake, let them see that it's an opportunity to learn and the mistake won't be repeated. Encourage people to admit their mistakes and actively demonstrate that they have learnt from them (this is a good general practice anyway): 'I arranged the meeting over a month ago and wrote it in the diary, but I never called back to confirm because the arrangement had been definite. I hadn't thought that the customer might change their schedule and forget to tell me. Still, after wasting an hour and a half travelling to see someone who wasn't there, that's one mistake I shan't make again. I'm going to confirm every appointment I ever make from now on.' This kind of self-assessment will give the control freak confidence that the lesson really has sunk in.

- (▶) As team leader, you can sit these people down and ask them what the worst possible scenario is if someone does mess up. Often it's not really that bad, and getting them to verbalize it helps them to see it in perspective.

- (▶) If you have people on the team who are prone to make the kind of mistakes the control freak hates, don't invite trouble by asking them to work closely together.

- (▶) Once a control freak has learnt to trust someone, you should find that they become excellent at delegating – at least to that person – and they'll be more open-minded about learning to trust someone else after a happy experience last time. So try to put them together with one of the most reliable team members while you're unofficially training them to trust their colleagues more.

If you have people on the team who are prone to make the kind of mistakes the control freak hates, don't invite trouble by asking them to work closely together

THE KNOW-ALL

Know-alls are infuriating. You find yourself wanting them to be wrong even though the project and the team will suffer – and that's not healthy. But how do you stop them frustrating everyone?

 Know-alls are incapable of saying 'I was wrong.' Rather than pointing out their errors to them, ask them to explain their ideas or plans to you so that they can spot their own mistakes as they speak. If they don't identify them, ask them questions that focus on the area you feel needs closer examination.

 Don't try to humiliate them in front of other people, tempting though it may be – you will only antagonize them.

 Give them credit where it's due, but make them share it: 'That was a very good idea, Pat. Mind you, we'd never have got the results we did from it without Jason's inspired planning. And Jacky's presentation was first class.' Make sure the know-all recognizes everyone else's contributions as well as their own.

thinking smart

CONFIDENCE BOOST

Know-alls tend to knock people's confidence by crediting themselves with every good idea and every success. So keep everyone else's confidence boosted – particularly those who work closely with the know-all.

76

THE PRIMA DONNA

It's no coincidence that these people are prone to act like five-year-olds. This kind of behaviour is usually learned in early childhood; they discover that by creating a scene they can get what they want. In a work environment, however, you want people to focus on what is the best way to achieve the team's objectives, not on fulfilling their personal agenda.

- ▶ **The prima donna has learnt that this kind of behaviour gets them what they want. All you have to do is to teach them that it doesn't – at least not here. It may take time after years of finding it successful, but if you're consistent they'll learn in the end.**

- ▶ **Don't respond to this kind of behaviour. Find an excuse to leave the room – make a phone call or grab a coffee – and come back when they've calmed down. Be responsive and willing to listen as soon as they're calm and rational, but opt out of the conversation whenever they become childish.**

- ▶ **Don't meet their emotion with emotion of your own: meet it with cool, objective, factual statements and information-seeking questions.**

THE ROWDY PERSON

They sing to themselves while they're waiting for the phone to be answered, they burp loudly, they laugh uproariously at things they're reading to themselves – in short, they're cheerful, jolly and

Don't try to humiliate a know-all in front of other people, tempting though it maybe – you will only antagonize them

well meaning, and their colleagues are frustrated, irritable and underproductive.

▶ It can help to have an informal word with these people. They generally have no idea that they are disrupting everyone; often they think they're being helpful in keeping everyone's spirits up. So be positive in your approach: 'It's great to have someone cheerful and optimistic around, especially when things start to get a bit pressured. The only trouble is ... '

▶ If the problem doesn't diminish after this, the best solution can be to put physical distance between this person and the rest of the team. Put them in the corner of an open-plan office, or give them their own room if you have individual offices. It might be more tactful to give a different explanation for doing this. Instead of squashing their zest for life by saying 'No one wants to sit near you,' you could say, 'It makes sense for you to be nearer the fax machine' or 'you meet a lot of customers at the offices – you really need your own room.'

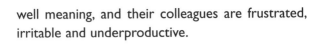

thinking smart

IT'S AN ILL WIND

You can't change these people's natural ebullience, and you really shouldn't try. There are times when it is exactly what the team needs. These are the people who keep everyone's spirits up in a crisis.

THE OVERCOMPETITIVE PERSON

Colleagues competing with each other can work well if it's done on a friendly level, and especially if there's an element of luck involved – such as who happens to answer the phone to the customer placing the huge order. It can spur people on and help keep them motivated. But overcompetitiveness can be very destructive, as well as being demoralizing to anyone who can't keep up and so always loses.

▶ Concentrate on focusing the team's performance on its customers (whether they are internal or external), not on each other. Explain to the team collectively (in a friendly, informal way) that you'd like them to channel their competitive drive outwards rather than inwards.

▶ If an overcompetitive person can't ease up, try to encourage them to compete against themselves and beat their own targets.

▶ Occasionally, someone takes competitiveness so seriously that they start to keep back information from other members of the team in order to give themselves a competitive advantage over them. This does the team immeasurable damage and you will have to speak directly to the person about it explaining why it is bad for the team.

▶ A few people are born so competitively natured that they just can't help it. If nothing else works, your best option might be to allocate them tasks where they work independently and therefore have nothing to compete over.

THE BULLY

Bullying within the team destroys any chance of real team spirit, and it needs to be controlled. Of course, you can't eradicate it completely. That's all right, you just need to reduce it to a level where the rest of the team can handle it.

- Domineering people often pick on the weakest person around – often the youngest, least experienced member of the team. Stand up for this person until they learn to stand up for themselves. Don't be aggressive in their defence, or confrontational, but don't allow the domineering person to bully them. If they are trying to dragoon them into doing an urgent task that they don't have time for, come to their support and say, 'Actually, Peter has got his priorities right. The research he's doing for Jacky is very urgent and he can't do anything else until he's completed that.'

- Domineering people tend to try and shout other people down. Don't react. If everyone else stays calm, they will start to look rather silly losing their cool. They'll soon learn to stay in control rather than make a fool of themselves.

THE AGGRESSIVE TYPE

This type of person can upset other team members. Aggressive people tend to think and act fast, and they are often insecure and need recognition and personal power. These aspects of their make-up can guide you in dealing with them.

- Because they like to get on with things, it eases your relationship with them if you can move at their speed on projects you're working closely with them on.

- They need recognition and will sometimes put people down in order to make themselves appear superior. If you give them credit when they deserve it they won't need to do this.

THE MANIPULATOR

Good manipulators never leave any evidence; you can't actually *prove* that they've been manipulative. But you know it anyway. And so does everyone else. There's no point challenging them directly because they'll deny it. So make them feel that you want to help, not to point the finger.

- If they are manipulating a situation, they must have a reason. Think it through and work out what they are trying to achieve.

thinking smart

ASSERTIVENESS PAYS

Aggressive people don't necessarily want you to capitulate to them all the time – they often don't like people who are wet. They would much rather be able to respect you. So stand up to them assertively (but non-aggressively) when you need to.

▶ Talk to them without accusing them of manipulation: 'I get the feeling that you'd like to run the ABC Ltd account. Is that right?'

▶ They will probably agree with you, but if they deny it give them reasons why you have this impression. 'I noticed at the meeting last Thursday that you highlighted one or two errors that Pat had made recently with the account. You don't normally focus on that kind of detail unless you have a particular interest in the subject – so I concluded that you were probably interested in the ABC account.'

▶ Once the manipulator feels they can talk confidentially and openly to you, without fear of accusations of manipulation, they will do so. After all, they are more likely to achieve their aim that way.

▶ If you can't give them what they want, explain the reasons to them. 'Pat is running the account well, albeit a little differently from the way you would do it. And the customers are happy and settled; I don't want them to have to get used to a new contact person here when it's not necessary.' But compromise with them if you can: 'If you feel you're ready to handle larger accounts, though, we can talk about finding a suitable large account for you to take responsibility for.'

THE RULE BENDER

Rule benders often get excellent results by playing the system or ignoring a few minor regulations – that's why they do it: because it works. These people are a problem for two reasons. One is that the team

– or even the company – can be in trouble if their rule bending is uncovered; the other is that the rest of the team resent their getting away with it.

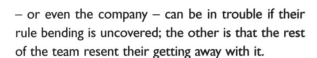

DON'T MAKE ASSUMPTIONS

Before you tackle the rule bender, make sure they don't have a valid point. They may be breaking a rule of the team's own making that is better broken – so always make sure the best solution isn't to abolish the rule.

▶ Assuming this isn't the case, stand up to them for the sake of their colleagues. Resist their argument that their results improve when they bend the rules.

▶ If they agree to play by the book, give them at least as much recognition and reward for good results, even if the results aren't quite as good as they were when the rules were being bent. This should reduce their need to get results at all costs.

▶ Bring up the matter at team meetings. Don't accuse the rule bender personally; just raise the issue of rules in general, or the particular one in question. If they see that their colleagues are opposed to their behaviour, they may think twice.

▶ Obviously, if you cannot stop this person from twisting the rules you may have to warn them that you will report them next time, or take disciplinary action.

THE BUCK PASSER

These people are full of excuses for not having done things: 'Robin was away so I couldn't get at the research material,' 'The computer went down on Tuesday,' 'Pat needed me to produce a report really urgently at the end of last week.' You're just waiting for them to say, 'The dog ate my homework.' These excuses often implicate other team members, which can lead to conflict within the team.

- Be very specific about the targets for tasks you give them to do. For example, 'I'd like this report to be fairly in-depth – say around 10,000 words – and I need it completed, printed and bound by 4.30 this Friday.' You may find that you need to put all instructions in writing for some buck passers.

- If they give you any excuses, just use the stuck record technique. If they tell you they couldn't get at the research material say: 'I can see that makes it harder. But I still need it on Friday.'

- Occasionally they may have a genuine problem in getting the work done, but don't help them unless it's really necessary, otherwise they'll never learn to sort out their own problems, and they'll always dump them on you. If they try to do this, stop them by responding to their excuse: 'I can see it's a problem for you not having access to the material you want; how are you going to solve it so you can still deliver on Friday?'

- If they try to blame someone else, don't get sidetracked. If they tell you Robin shouldn't have taken the key to the filing cabinet home, just say, 'That's a separate issue. At the moment we're talking about how you're going to deliver this report by Friday.'

- Make it clear that responsibility for something means being responsible no matter who actually does the work, and whether or not you're there at the time.

THE PUT-DOWN MERCHANT

These people like to belittle others by making snide remarks or ones that contain poorly concealed criticisms. They are full of remarks such as 'Late again, Kate? No surprises there,' or 'You actually managed to read it, did you? Mind you, I don't imagine you understood much of it.' If it's any consolation, other people aren't likely to take the implications seriously, since they will all be well aware of the type of person the comments are coming from. But how do you deal with it?

- The first thing is not to give them any ammunition. If you *are* always late, it's difficult to respond to the accusation, however unpleasantly they have chosen to put it. So make sure you give them no valid grounds for putting you down.

- If you rise to the bait, you will only create a row, which will get you nowhere. If you rile this person, they'll get worse and not better.

- If you respond submissively, on the other hand, you encourage them to carry on putting you and other people down. If you are happy to ignore the remarks with dignity, you can do so, but if you want them to stop, this isn't the way to go about it.

- So you're left with the rational centre course – assertiveness. Reply with a polite question that challenges the put down. When they say, 'Late again?' you reply, 'Apart from last Wednesday, when there was a tube strike, I don't believe I've been late for several months. Which occasion are you referring to?' This will take the wind out of their sails and you'll find, if you employ this technique regularly, they'll soon learn that if they try to belittle you, it's them who will end up looking foolish.

Just remember that you can't change people's personalities. Once you accept that, you stop expecting miracles and you find you're satisfied with a reasonable improvement. Once you have the basic techniques under your belt, difficult people suddenly don't seem nearly so difficult after all.

for next time

As soon as you think you recognize one of these types in a colleague, a team member or a boss, look up the relevant section and learn how to deal with them from the off. You will always get results faster if you start out as you mean to continue, rather than changing your technique later on.

Just remember that you can't change people's personalities

difficult people in five minutes

You're off to a meeting, and you've just discovered that Valerie is going to be there. That's Valerie, the snide, sarcastic one. Or maybe you've got to discipline whinging Walter in five minutes. Or perhaps you've just been called into bully-boy Ben's office.

So what are you going to do? You've got five minutes to prepare yourself for an encounter with a prime example of a difficult person. Now just keep calm. Five minutes is plenty of time to get ready. Here's what you have to do:

- ▶ Remind yourself that they are the difficult one, not you. What's more, everyone else knows that too.

- ▶ You need to stay calm when the time comes. If you are worried that you're going to lose your rag or burst into tears, try promising yourself a real treat on the condition you manage to keep your cool.

- ▶ See if the problem type is included in Chapter 6. If so, look up the technique for dealing with them.

- ▶ Remind yourself of the guidelines for assertive behaviour (page 20).

- ▶ If the problem is your boss, refresh your memory by looking through the relevant parts of Chapter 4.

- ▶ Whatever the difficult type, think about the reasons why they are difficult (you may find Chapter 6 enlightening on this point). Simply seeing the other person's point of view can make them far less frustrating, irritating or intimidating.

- ▶ If you're dealing with someone overbearing and you still feel nervous after all this, just try imagining them being given a rollicking by the MD (or if they are the MD, by a very important customer). It usually helps to put things in perspective.